Awake My Soul
Presents

The Awake 5 Step Morning Routine and Devotional Companion

A Christian Life Coach Project
With CorrieLeeAnn and Friends

Copyright © Corrie Barnett, 2019
Photography © VickieLynnPhotography, 2019
Published and Edited by Corrie Barnett
ISBN: **9781090347367**
All rights reserved.

Contents

	Acknowledgments	ii
1	Introduction	iii
2	Five-Step Morning routine	vi
3	Day 1-5 with CorrieLeeAnn	Pg #21
4	Day 6-10 with Lindsey Ford	Pg #33
5	Day 11-15 with Whitney Caudill	Pg #45
6	Day 16-20 with Vickie Barnett	Pg #57
7	Day 21-25 With Corey Johnson	Pg #69
8	Day 26-30 with Shanna Lanning	Pg #81
9	Graphic Organizers	Pg #92

Acknowledgments

A life time of experience and a few years of dreaming/goal planning with some amazing friends has made this project possible. I have so many "great ideas" and I need to thank my family. Mom, Dad, Cole, Nikki... you've listened to them all and I mean THEM ALL. Shanna, Corey, Mom, Whitney and Lindsey, you all have contributed to my life's journey in priceless ways and now I'm so excited to share those perspectives with the world. You are among the truest friends a girl could be blessed to have. Dad, for the drives to the studio; Cole for the countless tuning and editing hours you've put in; Erik, for the amazing background vocal arrangements; Anna for your genuine support; Jack for the tireless efforts you've spent mixing and tuning... John for your vocal contribution (Michael Bolton Who?) It's been an honor to create the content of this program with you and the fact that we are all like-minded in wanting to just share Jesus and the love we've found in Him...well, that's icing on the cake. #settheworldonfire

Introduction

Good morning and welcome to your guide to the 5-step morning routine that is designed to help restore your body, soul and spirit the way God intended. "in balance". To quote an article from the Entrepreneur, science teaches us that the first 20 minutes after we wake up is called the alpha cycle. It's been called the gateway to the subconscious mind. It's the window when your mind is the most impressionable and soaks up information like a sponge.

God's word has a lot to say about morning routines as well. To name a few things: In Psalms, we read that His lovingkindness, His steadfast love and joy is waiting for us in the morning. In a quick google search, I found over 90 verses where morning is mentioned. Through this book, I'm going to present to you a tried and true morning routine, used by some of the world's top successful people. These routines will encompass self-care for your body, soul and spirit and the best part is that it can be done in the first 20 minutes of waking up. Although, don't be confined to the time frame or order. Make this your own. Even just making these things part of your day in some way will bring delight to your life.

This guide will combine scientific based research with inspiration from the Scriptures, and to top it all off we even have an audio version of these steps combined with a five song EP. My friends and I hope you'll check it out and that you are blessed by the songs we put together.

Well that's all for the intro, let's get started. Wake up, Beauty; it's time to Beast. Pour yourself a cup of ambition. We're not drinking coffee to wake up. We're waking up to drink coffee. Run the day or the day will run you. Purpose is an incredible alarm clock. It's not time to Namastae....in bed.

Step 1
Awaken the Senses

Did you know that setting a timer for your coffee maker could be exactly what your body needs to wake up in the mornings, according to a new study from the Journal of Environmental Psychology? That's because smelling the coffee can stimulate your appetite and raise your awareness levels. Frying bacon can do the same. However, that auto feature is not available on most kitchen appliances.

The scriptures give us many affirmations about the five senses. "Taste and See that the Lord is good"... "Faith cometh by hearing"... The five senses are what God has given us to explore this great world, and taking time to wake each of them can be a key component to carrying out your purpose with joy. You'll be setting yourself up to be in full alert mode at the start of your day. Some examples for waking up the senses are: **Touch.** Let your feet touch a cold tile floor. **Taste.** Just a taste of water can wake up your digestive system. **Sight.** Open the windows so you can see the sunrise as you prepare for your day. **Hearing.** Did you know that hearing just the right song can put you into a perfect mood for the day?

In fact, recently the streaming service Spotify teamed up with music psychologist, David M. Greenberg, to identify the ultimate "Wake Up" playlist. He says there are three things you should look for in songs to help you wake up in the morning. 1. They should be songs that build, and start gently, even if it's for a few seconds. 2. They should be positive. 3. They should have strong beats.

God has made our body with its own rhythm, pattern, and a prewired way of working. When you take time to wake up each of your senses you encourage your body to get on board with the design you were created with.

Psalm 59:16 says "But I will sing of thy power; yea, I will sing aloud of thy mercy in the morning." As you begin to awaken your senses, enjoy a nice tune. I suggest "Happy Am I" from the Awake My Soul gospel playlist album. ☺

Step 2
Whisper Your Heart to God

Be honest! How many of you have a current morning routine that consists of the first 10 minutes lying in bed thinking about how tired you are. Or, maybe you wake up thinking… "The best part of waking up… is still a mystery to me." Well here's some hard, cold truth for you (if you can handle it). It's time to stop letting the day run you, and take control of the day… And that's exactly what happens when we take time in the morning to whisper our heart to God.

What exactly does that mean… whisper your heart to God? It can mean anything from praying, journaling things that you're grateful for, reading bible verses that remind you of your identity (we call these Scripture affirmations - I really like the one that says "I'm fearfully and wonderfully made") Whatever it takes for you to quiet your mind and remind yourself that you, not your thoughts, are in control.

I believe that this is such a vital step in awakening our souls that I have created organizers as part of this program for journaling, praying, collecting scripture affirmations in a quick convenient way. It really takes just a couple of minutes in the morning.

Why do this in the morning? Biblical Counselor, Darryl Burling says that having this time in the morning is important because it's the time you have the most control over. We think most clearly in the mornings and it sets up the rest of your day. In Psalms 90 we see the nature of God as one who wants to satisfy us in the morning with steadfast love so that we rejoice in our day.

I've heard it said that if you win the morning, you win the day. In my opinion, if you win the day, you'll win at life. In Col. 1:9-12 it reveals the key to a great life is simply asking God to reveal to us His knowledge and we're promised He'll direct our path.

What are some of the scientific and spiritual benefits? Just google "journaling and gratitude's effects on the brain" and you're going to get thousands of recent articles that show that just by spending 5 minutes a day praying… or listing 3 things you're grateful for can begin to rewire your negative thoughts and create a positive mindset. The physical benefits are that depression, stress, and anxiety are reduced by staggering amounts. Scripture refers to this as **being transformed by the renewing of your mind.** If you struggle with these emotions, journaling will help you think through those thoughts rationally. Partner this with using scripture affirmations to remind you of who God created you to be and, friends, you'll find yourself again. Better yet, you'll find who God meant for you to be, maybe for the first time. There is no better quench for your thirsty soul than can be found in your quiet place when you whisper your heart to God.

Step 3: Activate the Body

I never thought I'd be the type of person who would get up early in the morning to exercise and ... I was right. I have tried so hard, and maybe someday I'll get victory, but I began to feel some hope with this next fascinating fact.

Scientists have found that getting the blood and oxygen flowing for even just four minutes will activate your metabolism and create even, long lasting energy for your day. Four minutes? How does that work?

I was listening to a popular health podcast recently in which a workout trainer broke down the science behind the Japanese art of the Tabata workout. This training consists of 20 seconds of high-intensity exercise with 10 seconds rest, 20 seconds of low intensity exercise and repeat the pattern for 4 minutes. Working out in this way for 4 minutes can continue to have an impact on your metabolism for up to 30 hours afterward.

However, if that's not your thing, you can always just try dancing like no body's watching.

In the daily devotion portion of this book, we have a suggested 4-minute workout routine for each week, *but of course check with your Doctor first to make sure it is suitable for you.*

In the scriptures, the Bible talks about how exercise profits the body little, but hey... it does profit.

Activating the body in this way will allow you to not only have energy for the first part of your day... but for all of your day. As you choose which way you are going to activate the body as part of your morning routine, I'll leave you with this quote to think about. "She wakes up with grace in her heart and fire in her soul."

Step 4
Kick Negativity to the Curb

We can't expect to live a positive life with a negative mind. In step two of our routine called, "Whisper your heart to God," we began to see how we can rewire and renew our mind but sometimes it's as much prevention as it is the cure.

In the first moments of the day, remember that this is the time you control. It's the time that you get to remind yourself of who you are. It's not yet time for the outside world. Let's go through a list of do's and don'ts for the first part of your morning…Don't Check email - Don't Look at Social Media - Don't Listen to the news. (that will all be waiting for you once you've had your quiet time). Do Listen to a podcast, inspiring message, TED talk, audio book, or read - Do Fill your brain with positive thoughts and ideas to improve yourself. Take this time to learn the knowledge from the people who have done what you want to do.

I am also aware that as much as we try to avoid it, sometimes our lives may be overshadowed with negativity that no amount of planning or prevention can counteract. It can hang over our head like a dark cloud that overtakes our mindset.

In the midst of a trial like this, we have two choices… let the negativity rush over us and fall at its defeat, or we can choose to believe that God is working out something great in our lives through this valley. This is where we use one of our Scripture affirmations. The scripture I like to read when negative situations are out of my control reminds me that "I Am Not Alone". It's found in Psalms 139. "If I ascend up into heaven, Thou *art* there; if I make my bed in {hell}, behold, Thou *art there*. If I take the wings of the morning, *and* dwell in the uttermost parts of the sea, Even there shall Thy hand lead me, (are you starting to get the picture here) and Thy right hand shall hold me. If I say, Surely the darkness shall cover me; even the night shall be light about me. Yea, the darkness hideth not from Thee; but the night shineth as the day; the darkness and the light *are* both alike *to* Thee." God sees the whole picture, and no matter what we are going through, we are not alone.

Step 5
Embrace the Journey

==Every morning you have two choices: continue to sleep with your dreams or wake up and chase them.==

I personally know what it's like to feel like you are sitting on the sidelines of your own life. It's easy to feel defeated that your dreams aren't coming true. You have all these great ideas and expectation, but you work so much or feel so many disappointments in life that there's no way you can accomplish it all so...why try. So you say to yourself "I'll Just go with the flow...be comfortable...doesn't everyone live with a small amount of regret?" If that's you, I've been there, friend. A few years back, something inside me began to stir as if I was hearing a voice shout..."WAKE UP, Corrie!" Was it an audible voice? No, it was much louder than that. It all started when I began visualizing some things I wanted to happen that were beyond myself, which gave me an inner motivation, a drive, and eventually, it led me to action. (that's the psychological explanation anyway) It wasn't easy I had to overcome fear. I found encouragement in Romans 4:20 and 21 where I was reminded that Abraham didn't waiver from his beliefs. He knew that God would perform what He had promised him so he continued on his journey. He tapped into confidence beyond himself, and his confidence was anchored in what he believed God had for his life.

Creating this very project and the projects to come started as a dream for me. I had to come to the place that even if my measure of success was just to create, just to go through the process, I couldn't live without trying anymore. Another amazing thing began to happen as I started creating. I began to realize that this dream wasn't about me anymore. It became about my calling. It became about my life's purpose to encourage others and to share the healing and love that could take them out of despair like it had me. It's not been an easy journey. Before my dreams could become a reality I had to put together a plan. I wanted to be out of debt so I began a small online boutique business that helped me pay off student loans. I began writing songs that I didn't have a purpose for at the time but knew God had put them on my heart for some reason; and I began practicing my life coach talks on my 6th graders. Even though it wasn't time for the dream to become a reality, I can't explain it, but ==just by simply preparing for it, something began to wake up deep within my soul.==

It reminds me of the prophecy from the Old Testament, when Ezekiel went to the Valley of Dry Bones. God gave him a vision that the dead nation of Israel would come alive once again because God had a plan, He had a purpose. And though it took many years for that vision to become reality... it restored hope.

Life can be pretty interesting trying to make sense of it all (our calling, our dreams, our wants, our disappointments). I've adopted this as my Life's motto "==Don't forget to enjoy the journey==" because ==the joy has been in the process.==

How about you? Do you feel like you have lost your spark for life? ==Have you chosen to sleep with your dreams instead of chase them?== *yes!* I want to encourage you to keep your dreams fresh, even when it's not yet time to be in the position at work you want, or give life to all of your great ideas, or maybe just have those shiplap walls you've always wanted installed in your kitchen. I want to encourage you that this… is your planning time, friend. So create that Pinterest board, and start pinning. Believe it will happen and use this time for preparation. If you find any of this relatable then God gave me this project for the both of us.

God has a plan for you, and when we begin to believe it, we will set this world on fire. And, hey! Even if you don't believe it just yet, He'll believe it for you until you do as He begins his peaceful whisperings to your soul… *"Wake up… it's time… wake up!"* #awakemysoul

Devotion Companion

You have just read the Awake My Soul 5 Step Morning Routine with Christian Life Coach CorrieLeeAnn, and now it's time to get to work. The content you will read on the next pages will help you plan out your morning routine and encourage you for the first 30 days of your journey as you get into your new routine.

When creating a new routine, start small, and plan to reward yourself. Maybe buy that new coffee maker with the built-in timer to go off that will wake you up in the morning. This will speak to your brain sensors that what you're doing is bringing immediate pleasure until the long term benefits kick in.

I have invited some of my closest friends to help create a devotion of encouragement for the start of your journey. In addition, I have created useful organizers to help you continue the routine beyond the pages of this book.

Enjoy your journey to a better morning routine. A better sense of wholeness is just a few action steps away.

Corrie Barnett

About

CorrieLeeAnn
Camby, In
Preacher's Daughter
Elementary School Teacher
Business Owner

Hey beautiful souls, I'm CorrieLeeAnn (aka Corrie Barnett). I grew up as a preacher's daughter and lived on a bus, traveling and singing, with my family until I was 18 years old. For the past 10 years I've been teaching in public education for my home state of Indiana. On weekends I still enjoy singing with my family group, "The Barnett Trio." I'm so excited that I finally get to combine my two passions of music and teaching in this unique project. For fun, I enjoy traveling, photography, being a dog mom to my rescue Shih Tzu, Daisy May, and teaching my niece, new songs to sing. I also LOVE listening to podcasts for business ideas, and watching true crime documentaries... I could go on, Y'all, there is just too much to love about life. As you read these devotions for the next few days, please know, I've prayed for you. Just think of me as that cool younger or order sister you've always wanted. ☺ I'm rooting for you and believing in the steps you are taking to a lifestyle of wholeness. - LYLAS

Morning Routine
-Wake up to coffee brewing.
-Sit up and think of 3 simple things to be thankful for.
-Wash my Face.
-Currently practicing 4 minute yoga poses to stretch.
-Ask Alexa to Play my Flash Briefing (motivational skills).
-Prepare my coffee with MCT oil powder.
-Prepare my Xooma alkaline mineralized water, Vitamins, and B12 powder mix for the rest of morning. (this is life)
- Spend a few minutes reflecting on my current passion projects.

DAY 1

Scripture Affirmation

Write out your Scripture affirmation for the day below.
PSALM 34:8

Taste & see that the Lord is good. Oh, the joys of those who fear Him will have all they need.

Today's Thought Awaken Your Senses

We've all done it or had it done to us. You know the age old prank of "slipping a mickey". This took place for most of us at camp where a "friend" would pretend to bring you your favorite drink. As they came closer, you became desperate for how it was going to quench your thirst, but instead, when you drank it -your brain translated disgust. It could have been just water when you were expecting soda, but because your taste buds were prepared for something completely different, it might as well have been poison. This morning I encourage you to "taste and see" that the LORD is good. We are encouraged to taste first (put our trust in Him) and only then can we see (be enlightened and gain the knowledge) that He is up to good things in our lives. He has the greatest blessing in store for us. Be on the look-out for the flavor of the day... He's got something good that's guaranteed to quench our thirsty soul, even when life tries to "slip us one of those mickey's". #tasteandsee

Today's challenge

Try my favorite morning drink that is sure to be a delicious way to awaken your taste buds.

Shake up in a blender bottle
Warm to preference
Enjoy.

- 8 oz Premade Premier Protein Shake (Vanilla)
- 1 tsp of MCT oil Powder
- 1 Tbs. of Cocao Powder
- Add Sugar Free Peppermint Mocha Creamer

WHAT TASTE CAN YOU BE GRATEFUL FOR TODAY?

Water to drink - so places don't have fresh water.

What is One new thing you are looking forward to this Year?

Launching NC Mastermind Writer & the Farmer.

Activate *do tomorrow* / Check List

Routine
Legs

Walking Lunges – 20 sec
Faux Jump Rope – 20 sec
Sumo Squats – 20 Sec
Faux Jump Rope – 20 Sec
Glute Lunges – 20 sec
Faux Jump Rope – 20 sec
Repeat 1X

- ☐ Awaken your Senses
- ☐ Whisper your Heart
- ☐ Activate the Body
- ☐ Kick Negativity to the Curb
- ☐ Embrace the Journey

DAY 2

Scripture Affirmation

Write out your Scripture affirmation for the day below.
PSALM 143:8

Today's Thought — Whisper Your Heart to God

In the book "Historical Lights", Abraham Lincoln was quoted as saying "I should be the most presumptuous **blockhead**, if I for one day thought I could discharge these duties without the aid and enlightenment of One who is stronger and wiser than all others." One of the greatest leaders of our nation knew the power of meeting with God in the morning. Each of his decisions were made after consulting with the One in whom he trusted. It is said that President Lincoln wouldn't have a meeting or take a morning appointment until his meeting with GOD was completed first. Later in Lincoln's career, he became so well known for praying that he was asked to proclaim a National Day of Prayer on March 30, 1863. As I read our affirmation today, no wonder he put so much stock into his morning meeting. The Psalmist says that God has His lovingkindness waiting for us in the morning. Not only that, when we lift our souls to Him, He's ready to point the way for the day. Oh and sidenote…I looked up the word "blockhead" and it pretty much means "moron". Hashtag of the day #dontbeablockheadtalktoGodthismorning.

Today's challenge

During your quiet time this morning, Listen to the song, "In the morning when I rise, Give me Jesus"
-by Chris Tomlin

What do you get out of your talks with God in the morning?

WHAT IS ONE THING YOU WANT TO BE "KNOWN FOR"?

Activate Check List

Routine
Arms and Abs

Push ups – 20 sec
Mountain Climbers – 20 sec
V Sit Ups – 20 Sec
Mountain Climbers – 20 Sec
Plank – 20 sec
Mountain Climbers – 20 sec
Repeat 1X

- ☐ Awaken your Senses
- ☐ Whisper your Heart
- ☐ Activate the Body
- ☐ Kick Negativity to the Curb
- ☐ Embrace the Journey

Day 3

Scripture Affirmation

Write out your Scripture affirmation for the day below. 3 John 1:2

Today's Thought Activate the Body

Did someone say they needed to **exercise**? Or did they say they had some **extra fries**? I'll be there in a moment if it's the latter...but I digress... Have you ever had a workout partner? I've tried that a time or two, when schedules aligned for me to join a friend. If you've ever experienced that, you know a beautiful thing happens over time. You become equally and sometimes even more invested in the other person's success. You experience life, work and meet goals together and there will forever be a bond with that person. In our scripture affirmation this morning, we see John talking to his best friend with whom he had a bond just like that. As he greets his friend he says I hope everything is good with you, your health and that your soul prospereth. At first glance the word prospereth captured my attention. In this simple greeting we see that his desire is that his friend is not just doing well, it's not just a casual "hey how's it going", but he hopes that his friend is THRIVING mind, body and spirit. Sometimes all we need is a little encouragement from the right friend to keep us on the right health and wellness track.

Today's challenge

Is there a friend in your life that you've noticed has lost their luster. Maybe that's you, but the act of encouraging someone else, can be the very thing that helps YOUR soul thrive this morning. Tell someone you want to see them "Prosper" "Crush it" "Flourish"... You get the picture. #ihopeyouprosper

Who's a friend you can encourage today?

WHAT IS A PHYSICAL GOAL YOU HAVE FOR YOURSELF THIS WEEK??

Activate

Routine

Your Choice
Dance to your Favorite Song

Check List

- ❏ Awaken your Senses
- ❏ Whisper your Heart
- ❏ Activate the Body
- ❏ Kick Negativity to the Curb
- ❏ Embrace the Journey

DAY 4

Scripture Affirmation

Write out your Scripture affirmation for the day below. Phil 4:8

Today's Thought **Kick Negativity to the Curb**

Get ready to geek out with me this morning..." In a study conducted by a professor at Harvard, it was discovered that negativity has twice the impact on our memory recall than positive experiences. This is simply because our brains are more sensitive to negative emotions. For example, I've been a driver since I was 16. I've made many road trips with friends through the years, driven myself to work every day; but in the spring of 2018, I was hit by a drunk driver. Although everyone walked away without a scratch, our cars were totaled and our lives spared. Now, every time I get in the car to drive, I can't escape that memory and I just brace for it to happen again. One negative experience will forever change my life. But science also says that we can rewire our brains. I guess Paul figured that out, back in the day, when he wrote this morning's scripture affirmation. We are promised that if we think on the true, the pure, the lovely, and think on it enough....we can trade our negativity for peace.

Today's challenge

Think of two positive things about a negative situation you are dealing with right now. #doubleshotofpositivity

Write those positive thoughts here...

NAME ONE DREAM YOU HAVE THAT BRINGS UP NEGATIVE EMOTIONS.? WHAT IS A SCRIPTURE AFFIRMATION YOU CAN USE ON THAT SITUATION??

Activate

Routine
Arms and Abs

Push ups – 20 sec
Mountain Climbers – 20 sec
V Sit Ups – 20 Sec
Mountain Climbers – 20 Sec
Plank – 20 sec
Mountain Climbers – 20 sec
Repeat 1X

Check List

- ☐ Awaken your Senses
- ☐ Whisper your Heart
- ☐ Activate the Body
- ☐ Kick Negativity to the Curb
- ☐ Embrace the Journey

DAY 5

Scripture Affirmation

Write out your Scripture affirmation for the day below.
Romans 8:31-32

Today's Thought — Embrace the Journey

I was listening to a clip of the "Steve Harvey Show" on Facebook the other day and he told a very inspirational story. To paraphrase he said there was a single mother trying to make ends meet by waitressing at a local diner. The diner was about to go under when she offered to make one of her homemade pies. The owner allowed it, and the next day it got the customers talking, and they asked her to make more. Soon she had saved enough money from selling pies, that she was able to buy a restaurant-grade oven, and started making pies for more restaurants. Now we see "Marie Callendar" pies in every grocery store in America. When she passed away in 1995 she had earned approx. $126,000,000 from baking pies. This morning, be confident in your calling, purpose, and the visions that you have for sharing your abilities with the world. If He's before us... who can stand against us? Walk in the truth, that you were made on purpose for a purpose. The distance between your dreams and reality, is simply taking action. #madeforapurpose

Today's challenge
Think of a dream you have and give it a "date" today!

Name one time you invested yourself into a project and saw a positive Profitable outcome.

WHAT IS SOMETHING YOU DO THAT PUTS YOU IN "YOUR ZONE"?

Activate

Routine
Legs

Walking Lunges – 20 sec
Faux Jump Rope – 20 sec
Sumo Squats – 20 Sec
Faux Jump Rope – 20 Sec
Glute Lunges – 20 sec
Faux Jump Rope – 20 sec
Repeat 1X

Check List

- ☐ Awaken your Senses
- ☐ Whisper your Heart
- ☐ Activate the Body
- ☐ Kick Negativity to the Curb

Start Each Day with a grateful Heart

About

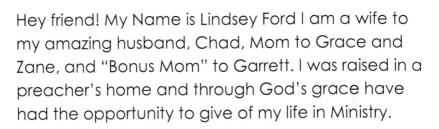

Lindsey Ford
MOUNT VERNON, OH
Wife, Mother, WorshipLeader, Writer, Entrepreneur

Hey friend! My Name is Lindsey Ford I am a wife to my amazing husband, Chad, Mom to Grace and Zane, and "Bonus Mom" to Garrett. I was raised in a preacher's home and through God's grace have had the opportunity to give of my life in Ministry.

I am a Worship Leader, songwriter, speaker, and professional shopper. ☺ I love to take a bargain and turn it into a profit! I'm a proud cancer survivor and am working daily to live a healthy, balanced life. I love to travel, shop, and spend time with friends and family. I look forward to connecting with you deeper over the next few days and trust God will work mightily in your life!

Morning routine:
-Before I get out of bed, express gratitude.
-Make coffee
-Do devotions
-Work out
-Get dressed and slay the day

Day 6

Scripture Affirmation

Write out your Scripture affirmation for the day below. Ps 119:18

Today's Thought — Awaken the Senses

I was driving home the other day and noticed a couple of "new" houses. The next time I was out with my husband, I pointed them out to him. After almost driving off the road, he looked at me with utter horror, a lot of shock, and a tinge of disappointment. You see, I've lived on this road for almost 30 years of my life, and never noticed those "new" houses? They were built long before I ever arrived. For the past 30 years, I have managed to be distracted, or just simply overlook what was right in front of me. Since that day, I have made it a point to look at my surroundings. (and you would not believe how many "new" houses I've found) When is the last time you looked for His blessings in your life? Birds chirping, wind on your face, sounds of a crackling fire, laughter of a child, ...or what about, fear, rejection, sickness... if we look, we can find Him in every circumstance. Through rejection, we find His acceptance. Through fear, we find His peace. Through sickness, we find His healing. May we open our eyes and behold the wonder of who Jesus truly is.

Today's challenge

Take a walk and look for the wondrous things He has created. The crunching leaves, bugs, flowers, clouds. Stop and thank the Lord for loving us enough to give us beauty all around! #activelylooking

What is a blessing you have missed seeing recently?

WHAT IS SOMETHING YOU CAN START NOW THAT WILL BE A BLESSING 30 YEARS FROM NOW ??

Activation

Routine
Legs

Glute Bridges – 20 sec
Side Shuffle – 20 sec
Leg Lift Left – 20 Sec
Side Shuffle – 20 Sec
Leg Lift Right – 20 sec
Side Shuffle – 20 sec
Repeat 1X

Check List

- ❑ Awaken your Senses
- ❑ Whisper your Heart
- ❑ Activate the Body
- ❑ Kick Negativity to the Curb
- ❑ Embrace the Journey

Day 7

Scripture Affirmation

Write out your Scripture affirmation for the day below.
Psalm 46:10

Today's Thought — **Whisper your heart to God**

We were made for one purpose. That purpose is to Worship our Creator. But, so often we're weighed down with baggage from our past, overwhelmed by the prospect of our future, and trying to "just make it" in our present.

I recently found myself preparing for a concert. While the event was something to glorify the name of Jesus, I was overwhelmed by nearly every decision "I" had to make. What I realized was, I had given so much of my time and energy into "creating" a worship experience, I had failed to spend quiet time with my Savior, allowing Him to create in me a spirit of worship. I was leading off of past experiences with the Lord, rather than serving from the overflow of His Holy Spirit in my life.

You see, I had become so busy "doing" I forgot to get busy "being". Being still, being vulnerable, being open to His presence, His prompting, His permissions.

When was the last time you were still? No TV, no phone, no social media, no agenda, just "still" before your Maker? Today, may we be still, and know that He is God.

Today's challenge

Journal a prayer, expressing where you want to be in your walk with the Lord, then "Be still" and allow Him to speak to your heart. #livingintheoverflow

Journal Here...

WHAT DID YOUR HEART HEAR HIM SAY??

Activate

Routine
Arms and Abs

Push ups – 20 sec
Mountain Climbers – 20 sec
V Sit Ups – 20 Sec
Mountain Climbers – 20 Sec
Plank – 20 sec
Mountain Climbers – 20 sec
Repeat 1X

Check List

- ☐ Awaken your Senses
- ☐ Whisper your Heart
- ☐ Activate the Body
- ☐ Kick Negativity to the Curb
- ☐ Embrace the Journey

DAY 8

Scripture Affirmation

Write out your Scripture affirmation for the day below. Romans 12:1

Today's Thought Activate the Body

When my son came home from school, he brought with him a jar that held a chrysalis. For the next several weeks, we checked the jar, just hoping "today would be the day" he would meet his beautiful butterfly. Then, tragedy struck... What once was a vibrant green chrysalis had turned jet black. I explained to Zane the butterfly had died and we would try again next year. But, oh, how wrong I was. You see, I didn't realize that before his butterfly could hatch, the chrysalis had to die. It was an ugly death. Full of darkness and unmentionable, slimy things. Yet, with persistence and time, that black covering fell off and the most beautiful life was brought forth. You may be in the chrysalis phase in your own life, feeling trapped by your current state, believing no one sees the effort you're making or changes you're trying to achieve... but, just keep dying! Die to your flesh, your cravings, your addictions, yourself, and before you know it, you will emerge as a new creature in Christ Jesus, ready to live the abundant life He has promised you! Go ahead and get busy dying so you can truly live!

Today's challenge

Gods Word tells us our body is a temple. We only have one. No second chances, no do-overs, this is it. Today, determine to cut something negative out of your life and implement with something positive (i.e. stop drinking soda. For each can you would typically drink, replace with one glass of lemon water) #dyingtolive

Can you recall something that "died" from which something new and beautiful formed?

WHAT IS ONE NEGATIVE HABIT YOU WILL WORK ON REPLACING THIS WEEK???

Activate

Your choice

Check List

- ☐ Awaken your Senses
- ☐ Whisper your Heart
- ☐ Activate the Body
- ☐ Kick Negativity to the Curb
- ☐ Embrace the Journey

DAY 9

Scripture Affirmation

Write out your Scripture affirmation for the day below. Phil. 4:8

Today's Thought Kick Negativity to the Curb

Have you ever had one of those days (or weeks, or even years?) where it seemed like nothing was going right? Sister, I have been there, and it's NO FUN! It's easy when life isn't "doing right" for Satan to try and steal our joy. But, does he not know who we are? We are daughters of the King, made in the image of our Creator, given a great purpose with a divine calling on our lives! So often we focus on "what if's". "What if I never get married?". "What if I don't get this promotion"? "What if I get sick"? "What if I lose a loved one"? Well, what if? If your worst case scenario happens, do you not serve a God who's big enough to handle each and every situation that comes His way? My Mamaw often says "What you can't control, commit". You can't control the world around you, but you can commit your actions and your thoughts to Him. Today, we focus on the "knows". We KNOW who our Savior is, and what His word promises. No matter what today brings, HE is still in control and HE will work things out for YOUR good!

Today's challenge

Instead of your list of "who done me wrongs" Start your list of "He done me rights" Let's kick that pity party to the curb and get our praise on! Start a praise list. Write down every praise you can think of and add to it throughout the day. You will be amazed at how you can praise yourself right out of the pit! #frompittopraise #raiseapraise

Start your Praise List here.

Activate

Routine
Arms and Abs

Push ups – 20 sec
Mountain Climbers – 20 sec
V Sit Ups – 20 Sec
Mountain Climbers – 20 Sec
Plank – 20 sec
Mountain Climbers – 20 sec
Repeat 1X

Check List

- ☐ Awaken your Senses
- ☐ Whisper your Heart
- ☐ Activate the Body
- ☐ Kick Negativity to the Curb
- ☐ Embrace the Journey

DAY 10

Scripture Affirmation

Write out your Scripture affirmation for the day below
Hebrews 12:1b

Today's Thought Embrace the Journey

Have you ever played "Tug-of-war"? You know, the miserable game when you're torn between putting all of your weight into it, pulling the rope to your side or giving in and being pulled to the opponents' side so everyone will be astonished at just how light you are? LOL! I wonder how often in life we play "Tug-of-war" with God? As He is trying to pull us to bigger and better things, we're holding on so tightly to what's comfortable. If only we would realize, He can't bring us higher if we're constantly holding on to what's bringing us down. I have felt so clearly God's calling on my life, as a worship leader, a wife, a mother, a writer, a speaker, yet, so often my hands are so full of worthless goals that I'm unable to take hold of whatever new opportunity He has for me. Don't wait for tomorrow. The time is now! Let go of your idea of what your life should be and surrender to your Creator. Allow Him to fashion each and every step you take, His ways are higher than yours and His plans are bigger than the biggest dreams you could ever dream!

Today's challenge

Make a list of items you want to remove (or limit) from your life. Whether it be physical clutter, emotional clutter or mental clutter, it's time to let go so He can take you towards your destination! #lettingoandlettinGod

List the top 3 things in your life that are causing clutter.

WHAT POSITIVE THINGS WILL HAPPEN ONCE YOU REMOVE THOSE THINGS??

Activate

Routine
Legs

Glute Bridges – 20 sec
Side Shuffle -20 sec
Leg Lift Left– 20 Sec
Side Shuffle – 20 Sec
Leg Lift Right – 20 sec
Side Shuffle – 20 sec
Repeat 1X

Check List

- ☐ Awaken your Senses
- ☐ Whisper your Heart
- ☐ Activate the Body
- ☐ Kick Negativity to the Curb
- ☐ Embrace the Journey

Corrie Barnett

I DID NOT wake up LIKE THIS.

About
Whitney Caudill

DAYTON, OHIO
FOUNDER OF HER STORY, INC.
THE CITY COFFEEHOUSE

Howdy Y'all! I am an entrepreneur and visionary who strives to create life changing opportunities for the glory of God and the good of others. It is my purpose in life to love and serve all people by creating community and a culture of belonging. I am a huge mental health and wellness advocate. I began my own journey of going from functional to optimal just a few months ago. I started seeing a therapist and it has added so much value to my life. She encouraged me to add the practice of daily gratitude to my morning routine and as a result, I feel more grounded and more at peace! I am honored to be a part of this project and I cannot wait to hear how it adds to your life!

MORNING ROUTINE

-Drink 4oz of green juice w/herb supplements (ashwagandha, eleuthero, ginkgo leaf & B12)
-Drink 1-2 cups of coffee & write/reflect in gratitude journal
-Check email
-40-minute workout while listening to a mental health podcast
-Create content and attend scheduled meeting

DAY 11

Scripture Affirmation

Write out your Scripture affirmation for the day below.
Lamentations 3:22-23

Today's Thought Awaken your Senses

Do you notice the morning sunrise? It's my favorite; a beautiful reminder of God's steadfast love and His mercies that never cease. So many of us love these words, maybe because on our darkest days they help sustain our hearts. But do we really sit and meditate on the incredible truth behind them?

God knows how our anxious hearts worry about today and tomorrow, usually at the same time. He wants us to know that we do not have to bear tomorrow's burdens. Today's mercies are for today's troubles. In Matthew 6:34 it says, to not be anxious about tomorrow, tomorrow is going to take care of itself. We can rest in the assurance that God will renew our strength for any and every occasion. God declares to us in Revelation 21:5 the He's making all things new and He is working those new things together for your good (Romans 8:28).

Today's challenge

Take a peek outside at the rising sun and meditate for 3 minutes on the truth of God's new mercy for you this morning. Take a deep breathe in, release and repeat.

How do you feel when doing this? (grounded, calm, peace, etc.)

AT WHAT TIME TODAY WILL YOU TAKE A THREE MINUTE BREAK TO JUST BREATHE?

Activate

Routine
Legs

Walking Lunges – 20 sec
Faux Jump Rope – 20 sec
Sumo Squats – 20 Sec
Faux Jump Rope – 20 Sec
Glute Lunges – 20 sec
Faux Jump Rope – 20 sec
Repeat 1X

Check List

- ❑ Awaken your Senses
- ❑ Whisper your Heart
- ❑ Activate the Body
- ❑ Kick Negativity to the Curb
- ❑ Embrace the Journey

DAY 12

Scripture Affirmation

Write out your Scripture affirmation for the day below. Proverbs 17:22

Today's Thought — **Whisper Your Heart to God**

In <u>Man's Search for Meaning</u>, author Viktor Frankl wrote about his intimate and dreadful Holocaust experience. He found that meaning often came from the small choices of prisoners, that is, to maintain belief in human dignity in the midst of life's worst circumstances.

*"We who lived in concentration camps can remember the men who walked through the huts comforting others, giving away their last piece of bread. They may have been few in number, but they offer sufficient proof that everything can be taken from a man but one thing: the last of the human freedoms—**to choose one's attitude** in any given set of circumstances, to choose one's own way." - Viktor Frankl*

We live in a broken world that can discourage us at any given moment. The good news is that we have the power to choose how we think and react. One of the best ways to combat these negative emotions is to practice gratitude.

Today's challenge

Sit in silence and think about what the meaning of life is for you.

What is one way you can act upon this gratitude (writing a note, putting in a good review, telling someone how you appreciate them)?

HOW CAN "CHOOSING A DIFFERENT ATTITUDE" HELP YOU ACCOMPLISH A GOAL YOU ARE STUCK ON???

Activity

Routine
Arms and Abs

Push ups – 20 sec
Mountain Climbers – 20 sec
V Sit Ups – 20 Sec
Mountain Climbers – 20 Sec
Plank – 20 sec
Mountain Climbers – 20 sec
Repeat 1X

Check List

- ☐ Awaken your Senses
- ☐ Whisper your Heart
- ☐ Activate the Body
- ☐ Kick Negativity to the Curb
- ☐ Embrace the Journey

DAY 13

Scripture Affirmation
Write out your Scripture affirmation for the day below 1 Timothy 4:8

Today's Thought **Activate the Body**

When I started my journey as an entrepreneur, it required a lot of energy and deep, focused work. I would be so busy that I skipped meals and passed up on exercise. I would reach for the blueberry muffin or a bag of chips and call it a day. There was so much to get done and no time to think about food! This quickly resulted in fatigue and mindless hours of brain fog.

I recently listened to a podcast by Dr. David Puder, a psychiatrist and health expert. He spoke about **sensorium**, which is the total brain capacity for focusing, processing, and interpreting. He went on to say that "we all have a baseline level of brain function, and this can be optimized by several factors like good sleep, healthy diet, good amounts of exercise, good mental functions (like reading), meaningful relationships, and good spiritual practice."

Our brain is the control center for our bodies. One of the ways we steward them well is to live healthy lives. Being healthy and activating your body in these areas will impact every area of your life, including your walk with God.

Today's challenge

Be mindful about how you treat your body today.
What is one thing you can do to improve your nutrition today? #mindovermatter

What is one nutritional habit that you are thankful you started implementing?

WHAT HEALTHIER CHOICE CAN YOU COMMIT TO PUTTING INTO YOUR SCHEDULE THIS WEEK. (10 MINUTE WALK, ACTIVE LISTENING, BETTER SLEEP, ETC.)??

Activate

Your choice
Try some Yoga Poses and Stretch for the morning

Check List

- ☐ Awaken your Senses
- ☐ Whisper your Heart
- ☐ Activate the Body
- ☐ Kick Negativity to the Curb
- ☐ Embrace the Journey

DAY 14

Scripture Affirmation

Write out your Scripture affirmation for the day below. Romans 12:2

Today's Thought — Kick Negativity to the Curb

I admit, I can be a bit of a perfectionist and an "all or nothing" thinker. I naturally process things as black and white. For example, if a new opportunity at work comes up, I may think something like, "If I am not perfect at this, I should not try at all, because then I will fail completely." I am also good at "shoulding" on myself, saying this like "I should have already finished school or I should already have my own private practice."
These are called cognitive distortions, which are skewed perceptions of reality. When I find myself gravitating towards these patterns of thinking, I take a moment, sometimes grabbing my journal, I write down what I am thinking and rewrite a more accurate statement. For example, I could be thinking, "I am always messing up" and a more accurate statement would be "I messed up once but most of the time, I do it right."
Learning how to identify and process your cognitive distortions can help you see through a more realistic lens and kick negativity to the curb!

Today's challenge

Focus on your thoughts and responses to those thoughts today. #shouldingstopshere

Name something that brought you joy yesterday.

WHAT IS A COMMON NEGATIVE THOUGHT PATTERN YOU HAVE? ??WHAT IS A MORE ACCURATE THOUGHT OR STATEMENT???

Activate

Routine
Arms and Abs

Push ups – 20 sec
Mountain Climbers – 20 sec
V Sit Ups – 20 Sec
Mountain Climbers – 20 Sec
Plank – 20 sec
Mountain Climbers – 20 sec
Repeat 1X

Check List

- ☐ Awaken your Senses
- ☐ Whisper your Heart
- ☐ Activate the Body
- ☐ Kick Negativity to the Curb
- ☐ Embrace the Journey

DAY 15

Scripture Affirmation

Write out your Scripture affirmation for the day below Philippians 1:6

Today's Thought — Embrace the Journey

In Genesis, the Bible opens up with a virtual tour of the beginning of all things and this is how we are first introduced to God—the Creator. From the start of life's journey, He is creating. "God, like any good creator and entrepreneur, lays a foundation, and from there, works and perfects His art, which is full of purpose and meaning," (Jordan Raynor, author of Called to Create.) We, human beings, are unique because we bear the image and likeness of God! And when we create for His glory and the good of others, we are living inside God's intended design: that we would bear His creative image to the world. Whether you are on a journey as an entrepreneur, a mother, a teacher, a friend – you are a creator! Every time we make a decision or speak a word, we are creating something out of nothing. The really cool thing is that we are always becoming, evolving and as Christians, being sanctified to be more like Him. Our journey doesn't end when we've reached our goal. We either build off of it or start a new one. Embrace the journey and know that, He who started a good work in you will carry it on to completion (Philippians 1:6).

Today's challenge

Think about the journey you are on. List out your gifts, passions, talents, and abilities. #thejourneycontinues

Who is one person you can encourage today to use their gifts for good?

IN WHAT WAYS CAN YOU EXERCISE YOUR GIFTS THIS WEEK??

Activate

Routine
Legs

Walking Lunges – 20 sec
Faux Jump Rope – 20 sec
Sumo Squats – 20 Sec
Faux Jump Rope – 20 Sec
Glute Lunges – 20 sec
Faux Jump Rope – 20 sec
Repeat 1X

Check List

- ☐ Awaken your Senses
- ☐ Whisper your Heart
- ☐ Activate the Body
- ☐ Kick Negativity to the Curb
- ☐ Embrace the Journey

Vickie Barnett
FREEDOM, INDIANA
FAMILY FOCUSED/MINISTRY MINDED

Hello everyone, I received Christ as my Savior at the age of 9 and surrendered my life to the Lord at the age of 17. It was shortly after that I met the love of my life of 42 years Missions Evangelist Minister Harlan Barnett.

We have two grown children (son Cole & daughter Corrie). Our family traveled several years singing together in evangelism as my husband preached in revivals and camp meetings. Along with being a wife and mother I played the piano for our ministry and also homeschooled our children. I still enjoy playing the piano and singing with my husband as we continue in the Lord's work.

We have a precious granddaughter who calls me "Mimi." This May, by the mercy of God, I will be celebrating 20 years as a Breast Cancer Thriver. I enjoy photography, reading, long walks, cooking, sewing, and crafting.

My heart's desire is to encourage others and direct them to Christ.

Morning Routine

-Begins with daily vitamins, and a protein shake.
-I start my day with reading my bible and prayer.
-20 to 30 minutes of exercise. Usually 3 to 4 days a week.

DAY 16

Scripture Affirmation

Write out your Scripture affirmation for the day below Psalm 17:8

Today's Thought Awaken your Senses

This morning I want to remind you that "**You are the apple of God's eye**". Although that may look like a Hallmark Greeting card title, it was actually written by the Psalmist, David. The phrase "apple of my eye" refers to something or someone that one cherishes above all others. How important are we to God? We are "cherished." Think on that for a moment. "Cherished" means protected, adored, and cared for. For years my family traveled and sang in evangelism. We sang a song together called "He Loves Me Like I Was His Only Child." It explains that God is capable of loving each of us the same, but as if we were the only one to receive His attention. His eye guides us through every trial and every blessing. Even in the midst of unpleasant circumstances that can overwhelm us and take us by surprise, He <u>sees</u> us. Nothing will ever take HIM by surprise.

Today's challenge

Send one blessing in your life to a friend or post it on social media today and use the hashtag #appleofgodseye

Can you name a time or a situation when you undeniably felt God's favor in your life?

WHAT IS ONE THING YOU WANT TO BE LOVED FOR BY YOUR CREATOR??

Activate

Routine
Legs

Side Lunges – 20 sec
High Knees – 20 sec
Back Lunges – 20 Sec
High Knees – 20 Sec
Front Lunges – 20 sec
High Knees – 20 sec
Repeat 1X

Check List

- ☐ Awaken your Senses
- ☐ Whisper your Heart
- ☐ Activate the Body
- ☐ Kick Negativity to the Curb
- ☐ Embrace the Journey

DAY 17

Scripture Affirmation

Write out your Scripture affirmation for the day below. PSALM 126:3

Today's Thought — Whisper your Heart to God

I recently read the quote **"I still remember the days I prayed for the things I have now."** I couldn't help but reflect on all the answered prayers that I have seen down through the years. At the age of 40, I was diagnosed with aggressive breast cancer that was caught very early. Even though I knew God, was the source of my strength & my hope, I still faced a roller coaster of emotions as one can imagine.

I remember thinking at my lowest point during treatment, "God I do not feel you but I know you are there." I began to experience what the words "faith" and "trust" felt like in a trial. It was indeed a long journey of chemo and radiation. That was almost 20 years ago. I am grateful and blessed that the Lord has allowed me to witness many answered prayers since that diagnosis.

Today's challenge

What are you grateful for today? Listen to the song "Give Thanks with a Grateful Heart." May you experience an #attitudeofgratitude throughout your day.

As you reflect today, what is one thing you have now that you didn' t before you begin praying for it?

WHAT IS A PRAYER YOU NEED ANSWERED TO BE ABLE TO GET TO THE NEXT STEP IN A GOAL OR DREAM??

Activate

Routine
Arms and Abs

Wall Push Ups – 20 sec
Jog in Place – 20 sec
Crunches– 20 Sec
Jog in place – 20 Sec
Tricep Dips – 20 sec
Jog in place – 20 sec
Repeat 1X

Check List

- ☐ Awaken your Senses
- ☐ Whisper your Heart
- ☐ Activate the Body
- ☐ Kick Negativity to the Curb
- ☐ Embrace the Journey

DAY 18

Scripture Affirmation

Write out your Scripture affirmation for the day below. Psalm 90:12

Today's Thought Activate the Body

Our scripture affirmation reminds us that we need to fill our lives with things that give us longevity. There are three practical steps that help me to press toward that goal.

LIVE- Exercise gives my **body balance.** *I Timothy 4:8 - For bodily exercise profiteth little: but godliness is profitable unto all things.* **LAUGH-** Laughter is a **stress reliever.**
Proverbs 17:22 A merry heart doth good like a medicine.
LOVE- Keep's my **emotions in check.**
1 Peter 4:8 - *And above all things have fervent charity among yourselves: for charity shall cover the multitude of sins.*

All three are related directly to the body and are key to longevity of life. Living is much better if we can live it in a healthy body with proper diet and exercise. This has not been easy for me as I have faced many obstacles concerning my health.

When I am overwhelmed and my life has become disorganized I try to remember to Live Laugh and Love as a way to refocus.

Today's challenge

Take a moment to reflect on your lifestyle.
Focus on those areas that are in need of balance. What steps are needed for you to Live-Laugh-Love? #livelaughlove

When was the last time you laughed?

IS THERE ANYTHING IN YOUR LIFE THAT SEEMS OUT OF BALANCE?

Activate

Routine
Legs

Side Lunges – 20 sec
High Knees – 20 sec
Back Lunges – 20 Sec
High Knees – 20 Sec
Front Lunges – 20 sec
High Knees – 20 sec
Repeat 1X

Check List

- ☐ Awaken your Senses
- ☐ Whisper your Heart
- ☐ Activate the Body
- ☐ Kick Negativity to the Curb
- ☐ Embrace the Journey

DAY 19

Scripture Affirmation

Write out your Scripture affirmation for the day below Proverbs 25:11

Today's Thought Kick Negativity to the Curb

I will never forget a time when words were used in my life to create a much needed spark of positivity. In my later 30's I found myself in a place of deep seeded bitterness. I remember knowing as a preachers wife, I needed to have a better grasp on the situation, but I let it fester inside, instead of dealing with it. A friend of mine could sense that something wasn't right. She told me about a book that would eventually lead to my admission of the problem and a call to action to deal with the emotions I was holding on to. She simply followed a nudge in her heart to share something with me at just the right time. What a great example of our scripture affirmation for the day "A Word Fitly Spoken". It reminds me of one of my favorite bible characters, "the little maid", mentioned in II Kings. She was brave enough in the right moment to share a resource that would lead Naaman to receive his healing from an awful disease. Her courage, awareness and resources ultimately served someone in their greatest need. Just as our lives can be influenced by the words of others, our words can also influence others' lives.

Today's challenge

Reflect on a time when you've shared and received "A Word Fitly Spoken"

Who is someone that has made a positive impact on your life with their words.

NAME A RESOURCE YOU COULD SHARE WITH SOMEONE TO HELP ENCOURAGE THEM TOWARD THEIR DREAMS.

Activate

Routine
Arms and Abs

Wall Push Ups – 20 sec
Jog in Place – 20 sec
Crunches – 20 Sec
Jog in place – 20 Sec
Tricep Dips – 20 sec
Jog in place – 20 sec
Repeat 1X

Check List

- ☐ Awaken your Senses
- ☐ Whisper your Heart
- ☐ Activate the Body
- ☐ Kick Negativity to the Curb
- ☐ Embrace the Journey

DAY 20

Scripture Affirmation

Write out your Scripture affirmation for the day below. Phil 1:6

Today's Thought — Embrace the Journey

"Mrs. Barnett, there's been a tumor growing on your spine and if we don't remove it now, you will be paralyzed." I can still hear those words from the Dr. as if they were being spoken in my ear at this very moment. He went on to explain that it was a high-risk surgery and there were no guarantees that I would come through without any damage. I was so discouraged and overwhelmed. We had just found out that our first granddaughter was on the way and all I could think of was that she would never know what it was like to have the best of me. I can't explain the surge of emotions I went through but ultimately my faith in the journey and the plan God has for me, anchored my soul. See, I truly believe that my life is His. I knew whatever the outcome was, I would continue to give this journey my all because that's where he needed my journey to go. I'm so thankful, that the surgery was a success and even though I deal with back pain from the surgery, I'm able to function in life as normal. Today's scripture has kept my life on track in a way that when I face life changing circumstances I can tell the Lord, "I trust you, and I always will."

Today's challenge

Think about the unpleasant circumstances of your journey. Could you use a little more faith to take the next step? #trust

List a time when God gave you the strength to get through a tough situation?

WHAT FUTURE CIRCUMSTANCE CAN YOU COMMIT TO TRUSTING THE LORD AND HIS PLAN FOR, RIGHT NOW??

Activate

Routine
Legs

Side Lunges – 20 sec
High Knees – 20 sec
Back Lunges – 20 Sec
High Knees – 20 Sec
Front Lunges – 20 sec
High Knees – 20 sec
Repeat 1X

Check List

- ☐ Awaken your Senses
- ☐ Whisper your Heart
- ☐ Activate the Body
- ☐ Kick Negativity to the Curb
- ☐ Embrace the Journey

About
Corey Johnson

Mills River, NC
Photographer
Entrepreneur

Hey there! I am Corey Johnson & I am a huge coffee enthusiast. I am from the town of Mills River, NC where I work as a graphic designer, videographer, and photographer. When I am not designing, filming, taking photos, or sipping on coffee, I am playing violin and guitar, singing, and spending time with my family and friends. I hope these next few days of devotions both encourage and challenge you to become a better you.

MORNING ROUTINE
-Set my alarm at least 5 minutes earlier than i need to give me time to enjoy the first part of my day
-I have to start a cup of coffee
-Take a few minutes to exercise & get my heart pumping.
-I often find myself asking Alexa to turn on some encouraging music so I start off my day on a positive note.
-During this time of "AWAKE" I will be in an attitude of thanksgiving & prayer for my day, and for others.

DAY 21

Scripture Affirmation

Write out your Scripture affirmation for the day below.
Matthew 6:22

Today's Thought Awaken the Senses

They say the eyes are the window to the soul, and what we see truly does affect our outlook on life. Being born legally blind, my vision is more than just what I see, but rather a culmination of visual and emotional feelings. We often get so wrapped up in how we look, or how others visually perceive us. While this is important, the emotions that are felt when we look at ourselves & our lives are far more effective on our day than just the visual representations we see. I enjoy beginning my day by looking at inspirational art I have hanging in my room or seeing an old photo from the past that has a great emotional memory. I have found if you can fill your eyes with positivity in the morning, you are less likely to focus on those negative sights you may view through the day.

Today's challenge

Purpose that today you will find one item or photo that brings a positive emotion or memory to mind. Take that item and put it somewhere you will see it on a daily basis.

What is one of your favorite memories from last week?

WHAT IS A NEW MEMORY YOU WANT TO MAKE THIS MONTH??

Activate

Routine
Legs

Side Lunges – 20 sec
High Knees – 20 sec
Back Lunges – 20 Sec
High Knees – 20 Sec
Front Lunges – 20 sec
High Knees – 20 sec
Repeat 1X

Check List

- ☐ Awaken your Senses
- ☐ Whisper your Heart
- ☐ Activate the Body
- ☐ Kick Negativity to the Curb
- ☐ Embrace the Journey

DAY 22

Scripture Affirmation

Write out your Scripture affirmation for the day below.
Colossians 3:15

Today's Thought — Whisper Your Heart to God

Growing up, I always heard that no matter what is going on, there is ALWAYS something to be thankful for. It may be very noticeable, or a blessing in disguise, but no matter what it is, it is still something to be thankful for. If we would take time to verbally thank God for at least one of those blessings, our heart will begin to get into a mood of thanksgiving. With my own life, I have been through times where I was falling into the pit of the "ungrateful attitude". Nothing was going my way, and it seemed like everyone around me was receiving all these incredible opportunities, but I was stuck in the same boring routine. It wasn't until I stepped back and took time to remind myself of all the many blessings God placed in my life, like the unexpected free coffee from Starbucks, or the small victory over a certain guitar chord. Those moments were when I realized how greatly blessed I really was.

Today's challenge

Tell three people today something you are thankful for that involves them. Share the attitude of thankfulness. It can be contagious! #blessingindisguise

List those three people below

WHAT IS A SMALL VICTORY YOU WOULD LIKE TO SEE THIS MONTH?

Activate

Routine
Arms and Abs

Wall Push Ups – 20 sec
Jog in Place – 20 sec
Crunches – 20 Sec
Jog in place – 20 Sec
Tricep Dips – 20 sec
Jog in place – 20 sec
Repeat 1X

Check List

- ❑ Awaken your Senses
- ❑ Whisper your Heart
- ❑ Activate the Body
- ❑ Kick Negativity to the Curb
- ❑ Embrace the Journey

DAY 23

Scripture Affirmation

Write out your Scripture affirmation for the day below.
Deuteronomy 6:5

Today's Thought **Activate the Body**

Have you ever felt like you're physically there, but your mind is off somewhere taking its precious time to catch up to you and the current situation? I can answer, YES, on many different occasions. As we work through this devotional and try to better ourselves, our bodies need to be pushed to their full potential. I use to not care about my body, but there came a time when I just had a serious conversation with myself and said, "Corey, this has to stop! Your friends, family, and job deserve your best." I began watching what I ate and started becoming very active. I find if I can get in a 10 minute morning exercise, whether it be running on the treadmill, doing jumping jacks, or doing sit-ups, my brain and body work more cohesively together, and I am able to devote my all to any task that may come up. Once you start implementing these little steps in your life, you will start noticing a difference in how you can focus.

Today's challenge

As you complete your activation challenge this morning circle the number that relates to the scale of focus you had this morning after the routine 1 2 3 4 5

How do you feel after you exercise?

WRITE OUT A PHYSICAL HEALTH GOAL YOU HAVE THIS YEAR.

Activate

Your Choice

Check List

- ☐ Awaken your Senses
- ☐ Whisper your Heart
- ☐ Activate the Body
- ☐ Kick Negativity to the Curb
- ☐ Embrace the Journey

DAY 24

Scripture Affirmation

Write out your Scripture affirmation for the day below.
Psalm 139:14

Today's Thought — Kick Negativity to the Curb

I will begin by saying this. **Guys** are also affected by preconceived image standards put on by the world. Most times we hear of all these girls who want to change their looks because they want to "fit in". Guys do have those same feelings. I grew up being "judged" by my looks. I guess pale skin, white hair, and eyes with no pigment doesn't fit the cookie cutter image this world promotes. I use to want to look "normal", but I realized God made me to be my own masterpiece. I am unique, and one of a kind. To change yourself would be like wanting to replicate Da Vinci's Mona Lisa, but you're not Da Vinci. You would become a duplicate or copy of an original work of art. Instead of being a duplicate, embrace your own beauty, and become the masterpiece that God has made you to be. After all, original works of art are worth so much more than a cheap knock-off duplicate. Don't let those negative thoughts take up space in your head. If you fill those spaces with love of how God made you special, you won't have room for negativity.

Today's challenge

Find something you don't like about your appearance, and replace that thought with something you love about yourself. Replace that negativity with self-love. Remember you are Fearfully and Wonderfully Made.

Name 3 physical traits you are thankful for.

HOW CAN YOUR UNIQUE QUALITIES HELP YOU ACCOMPLISH THE DREAMS YOU HAVE??

Activate

**Routine
Arms and Abs**

Wall Push Ups – 20 sec
Jog in Place – 20 sec
Crunches – 20 Sec
Jog in place – 20 Sec
Tricep Dips – 20 sec
Jog in place – 20 sec
Repeat 1X

Check List

- ☐ Awaken your Senses
- ☐ Whisper your Heart
- ☐ Activate the Body
- ☐ Kick Negativity to the Curb
- ☐ Embrace the Journey

DAY 25

Scripture Affirmation

Write out your Scripture affirmation for the day below
Jeremiah 29:11

Today's Thought Embrace the Journey

"You're only here for a short visit. Don't hurry, don't worry. And be sure to smell the flowers along the way." Walter Hagen. Life is such a fragile thing. One minute you are here, and the next you are face to face with eternity. So often we travel through life worrying over the past, and stressing about the future. With this mindset, we miss so much that happens in our life. In 2018, I felt like I was working constantly, and had no time to devote to being with my family and friends, or even time for myself to recharge and develop skills. I made a New Year's resolution to focus more on today and not work my life away. After a few months of doing this, I can already tell a huge difference in my happiness. We truly don't know what tomorrow holds, so why not do everything we can today to make it the best day we have ever lived? I don't want to look back and regret all those days I was too busy to just enjoy life's journey.

Today's challenge

Do something different today! Whether it be driving a different route to work, trying a new flavor of coffee, or simply taking time to notice those around you, try something new!

What about your day makes you happy?

WHAT IS SOMETHING NEW THAT YOU WANT TO TRY TODAY??

Activate

Routine
Legs

Side Lunges – 20 sec
High Knees – 20 sec
Back Lunges – 20 Sec
High Knees – 20 Sec
Front Lunges – 20 sec
High Knees – 20 sec
Repeat 1X

Check List

- ❑ Awaken your Senses
- ❑ Whisper your Heart
- ❑ Activate the Body
- ❑ Kick Negativity to the Curb
- ❑ Embrace the Journey

Tomorrow IS ALWAYS FRESH *with no* MISTAKES IN IT

— ANNE OF GREEN GABLES

About

Shanna Lanning

PISGAH FOREST, NC
PASTOR'S DAUGHTER
MOTHER OF FOUR

Hey from a mountain girl way up in the Blue Ridge of Western North Carolina. A pastor's daughter for over 35 years, I am a product of God's Salvation, Mercy, and Grace alone. I am married to my high school sweetheart and we have four children under age 12. So parenting is what I do most. My background is in broadcasting and I still enjoy some part-time work. I also work seasonally for the board of elections in our county and help with a small vacation rental business my family owns. I love quotes and have a journal to record my favorite author's thoughts and sayings. I enjoy audiobooks since you can still wash dishes while you read. My husband and I teach adult Sunday school class and are heavily involved in our church. In my spare time, you will find me on a little league field watching my three boys play ball, at gymnastics class with my daughter, or at the local airport flying with my husband who is a private pilot. I pray this devotion speaks to your soul as it has spoken to mine.

MORNING ROUTINE:
-Walk straight to the windows, pull back the curtains, and stand for just a moment to wake up.
-Turn on the coffee pot and hit the large button for my French roast K cup.
-Grab my favorite mug and head to the couch where I have my Bible, journal, and devotion book in a basket close at hand.
-Make Bed

DAY 26

Scripture Affirmation

Write out your Scripture affirmation for the day below
2 Peter 1:19b

Today's Thought Awaken your Senses

It had been a long night. The baby was up several times, my two-year-old was coughing, my four-year-old had nightmares, and I stepped in my six-year-olds slime experiment on the way to the coffee pot. Have you ever had a night that, whatever your issues were, made you think, Thank God, I survived? It's life, isn't it? Sometimes just getting the fog out of your brain seems a monumental task. My grandmother and mother both observe a ritual of opening the blinds and drawing back the curtains every morning before anything else is done. And I have found that this has the most amazing power to transform my day. The sight of the day or morning star, which is actually Venus, in the predawn sky and a few moments to reflect on the true Day Star in our lives is a game changer for me, no matter how rough the night. Also the sun bright in the sky with its warm light on my skin first thing each day is invigorating. Even if it is raining, the light will be there. May He shine in your heart today. A fresh start. A new day!

Today's challenge

Plan a morning this week that you can watch the sun rise and watch for the morning star.

After looking out the window this morning answer this. What is one thing about nature that brings you peace?

WHAT DO YOU GET A CHANCE TO START FRESH TODAY??

Activate

Routine
Legs

Glute Bridges – 20 sec
Side Shuffle – 20 sec
Leg Lift Left – 20 Sec
Side Shuffle – 20 Sec
Leg Lift Right – 20 sec
Side Shuffle – 20 sec
Repeat 1X

Check List

- ☐ Awaken your Senses
- ☐ Whisper your Heart
- ☐ Activate the Body
- ☐ Kick Negativity to the Curb
- ☐ Embrace the Journey

DAY 27

Scripture Affirmation

Write out your Scripture affirmation for the day below 1 John 1:9

Today's Thought — **Whisper Your Heart to God**

Have you made a mistake that you were unable to make right or erase? Do you ever wish that life was in pencil? My friend had two small children who colored themselves with sharpie permanent markers, and when she entered the room, the kids were running around with no shirts, covered in permanent marker, screaming and laughing. However, when it came time to face the music and confess, their voices were barely above a whisper. Two weeks later, you could still see the remnants of their escapade. That's how it seems to go. Some mistakes last longer and are more noticeable than others. It's like they are in sharpie. No turning back. But scripture says because of Christ's love for us, because of His grace, we have the gift of confessing our sins and mistakes to Him each morning. To whisper our deepest fears and failures. And as if they were in pencil, He erases our past, and we stand flawless in His eyes. The only thing He has written in sharpie is His great love for you and for me. "Every saint has a past, and every sinner has a future" –Oscar Wilde. Know that He loves you today.

Today's challenge

Write out in permanent marker the word "Forgiven" or "He Loves Me" and place it where you'll see it when you pray.

What promise has God put in permanent marker for you?

WHAT IS ONE STEP YOU CAN TAKE TO MOVE FORWARD THROUGH A PAST MISTAKE??

Activate

Routine
Arms and Abs

Shoulder Press – 20 sec
Side Shuffle -20 sec
Push Up– 20 Sec
Side Shuffle – 20 Sec
Ab Bikes – 20 sec
Side Shuffle – 20 sec
Repeat 1X

Check List

- ☐ Awaken your Senses
- ☐ Whisper your Heart
- ☐ Activate the Body
- ☐ Kick Negativity to the Curb
- ☐ Embrace the Journey

DAY 28

Scripture Affirmation

Write out your Scripture affirmation for the day below PSALM 100:3

Today's Thought Activate the Body

"You don't have a soul. You are a soul. you have a body"-C.S. Lewis. Ah, so true, and yet how our body looks and feels often impacts our soul doesn't it? The food we give ourselves dramatically dictates our sense of well-being, and yet, over and over again, I am tempted by the double stuffed Oreo cookies instead of the spinach in the grocery store. Research suggests many of us are addicted to sugar and that it significantly lowers our immune systems. It would seem as if this information would be enough to make me steer clear of sweets and, yet, many days the battle against sugar is a struggle. Balance is key to most things in life. When we exercise self-discipline with food choices, it can spill over into other areas of life and help with our ability to deal with stress, anger, and discouragement. Leaning on God to strengthen your will power with daily food choices is a great way to reach your health goals. He cares about you and how you look and feel. After all, He made us for Himself. "Discipline is choosing between what you want now and what you want most"-Author Unknown

Today's challenge

Choose one day this week to go without eating any artificial foods or processed sugar. #yougotthisgirl

What's a Healthy Alternative to your guilty pleasure that you love?

WHEN IS THE NEXT TIME YOU COULD MAKE THAT FOR YOURSELF AS A TREAT???

Activate

Routine
Legs

Glute Bridges – 20 sec
Side Shuffle – 20 sec
Leg Lift Left – 20 Sec
Side Shuffle – 20 Sec
Leg Lift Right – 20 sec
Side Shuffle – 20 sec
Repeat 1X

Check List

- ☐ Awaken your Senses
- ☐ Whisper your Heart
- ☐ Activate the Body
- ☐ Kick Negativity to the Curb
- ☐ Embrace the Journey

DAY 29

Scripture Affirmation

Write out your Scripture affirmation for the day below II Cor. 12:9

Today's Thought — Kick Negativity to the Curb

You've hopefully known at least one gracious person in your life. Maybe it was your mentor, your grandmother, a co-worker, a friend. A person who could make you feel super special no matter what you were wearing or how you felt. Today there is often pressure from every side to do more, be more, have more. And often times we may find ourselves full of guilt rather than grace. We give in to pressure that we can't get it right, that somehow we don't measure up. Guilt is a tool the enemy uses to pulverize us, to say we are not enough. Not enough for our parents, our spouse, our children, our boss. Not enough for God. I have great news my friend; the enemy is a low down snake of a liar, #mountaingirltalk. You are ENOUGH! Remember that when your mind starts down that road of self-loathing and inferiority. No guilt, only grace. The grace we can give to each other in this life and God's amazing grace which makes His strength perfect in our weakness. "No one can make you feel inferior without your consent,"-Eleanor Roosevelt

Today's challenge

Text a person in your life who could use a reminder that they are enough!

Name 3 people you can go to for encouragement when you feel "you are not enough"

WHAT DO YOU SEE YOURSELF DOING THE NEXT TIME YOU FEEL GUILTY??

Activate

**Routine
Arms and Abs**

Shoulder Press – 20 sec
Side Shuffle -20 sec
Push Up– 20 Sec
Side Shuffle – 20 Sec
Ab Bikes – 20 sec
Side Shuffle – 20 sec
Repeat 1X

Check List

- ❏ Awaken your Senses
- ❏ Whisper your Heart
- ❏ Activate the Body
- ❏ Kick Negativity to the Curb
- ❏ Embrace the Journey

DAY 30

Scripture Affirmation

Write out your Scripture affirmation for the day below
Romans 8:38 &39

Today's Thought — Embrace the Journey

I once heard a successful older person say "You can't get to where I am until you walk where I've been." That statement has lasted a long time in my memory. Each of us has a destination. And that destination will be Heaven if you have accepted Christ as Savior. But we all have different paths to walk, different problems, and storms, and pleasures, and gladness. Sometimes we can lose sight of what is really important or feel that the darkness will overtake us. I like what Dr. Martin Luther King said "Only in darkness can you see the stars." Triumph and, yes, even tragedy may cross our paths. If in the darkness we will look for the stars, we will find them. God promises never to leave us or forsake us. And that nothing, no depth of despair or height of joy can separate us from the love of God. And today is your day, more steps in your journey, another chapter in your story. Go for it! He has got your back!

Today's challenge

Purposefully pray for God to guide your path towards fulfilling dream you feel He's leading you toward.

What tragedy or Trial have you gone through that has lead you to your current dreams?

WHERE DO YOU SEE YOUR JOURNEY GOING IN THE NEXT 5 YEARS??

Activate

Routine
Legs

Glute Bridges – 20 sec
Side Shuffle -20 sec
Leg Lift Left– 20 Sec
Side Shuffle – 20 Sec
Leg Lift Right – 20 sec
Side Shuffle – 20 sec
Repeat 1X

Check List

- ☐ Awaken your Senses
- ☐ Whisper your Heart
- ☐ Activate the Body
- ☐ Kick Negativity to the Curb
- ☐ Embrace the Journey

Awake Organizer

Design A morning routine that puts your mind, body and spirit in balance for the day.

How will you start your Morning?

Write out your 5 step Morning routine

A

W

A

K

E

Scripture Affirmations

Combat negativity with these promises for your life.
#kicknegativitytothecurb

Scripture Affirmations

Combat negativity with these promises

Negative Emotion	Positive Replacement	Scripture
Inadequate	Grace	2 Cor.12:9-10
Confused	Peace	1Cor.14:33
Withdrawn	Healing	Ps 147:3
Violated	Life	2 Cor. 4:8-10
Disrespected	Kindness	Prov.25:21-22
Resentful	Overcome	Rom.12:17-21
Critical	Humbleness	James 4:6
Betrayed	Love	Psalm 89:2
Let Down	Refuge	Psalms 34:8-9
Excluded	Presence	Heb. 13:5
Unfocused	Future	Prov. 4:25
Pressured	Limits	I Cor. 10:13
Anxiety	Love	1 John 4:18
Out of Control	Rest	Matthew 11:28

A Prayer Model

If Praying is new to you or you just never know quite what to say, use the "Acts Model." When we **A**dore our Creator, **C**onfess our sins, share our **T**hankfulness, our hearts are then tuned to ask for our wants and desires (**S**upplications) from a pure heart.
#whisperyourhearttogod

A	Adore Your Creator	
C	Confess the areas you have fallen short and need help improving in.	
T	What is something you can thank Him for?	
S	What are your Supplications (your desires and needs)	

Are you Glad?

In my 6th grade class I ask my students this every morning. They are asked to journal one thing for every letter in the word "Glad". The catch is that what they list has to have happened in the past 24hrs. After practicing this, you'll soon begin to look for these things throughout the day. You'll be surprised at the positive perspective this brings. #kicknegativitytothecurb

G: One thing you're Grateful for
L: One thing you've Learned Today
A: One thing you've Accomplished Today
D: One thing you've Delighted in Today

Dream Organizer

A dream with a date becomes a goal. A goal with a plan becomes an action step. An action step carried out becomes REALITY. Here are some organizers to help make your life-purpose-dreams, a reality.
#embracethejourney

Dream

Date

Goals

Goal

Date

Action Steps

Monthly Planner

January	February	March

April	May	June

July	August	September

October	November	December

Thank you

Thank you, reader, for making the investment of your time to read these valuable truths that have made my day-to-day life just a little more meaningful. My prayer is that the heart, soul and passion this project was created with, inspires you to carry out your purpose with joy. I want to invite you to join our Awake My Soul Community.

- Website: www.corrieleeanns.com

- Facebook: Awake My Soul – with CorrieLeeAnn

- Instagram: Corrie_Barnett

We are sharing live interviews of the writers and musicians on this project and engaging members for authentic community there. More courses to come, stick with us, we're just getting warmed up.

Do you have the other products that go along with this program? Here's what's available at corrieleeanns.com

- CD: Audio Version of the Program with 5 New Gospel Tunes
- Book: The Program and 30 Day Devotional Companion
- Book: The Awake 3 Minute Journal
- Downloadable Audio Files and PDF books
- Small Group/Sunday School Material

REFERENCES

- **Safwan, Ahmed. 2017 July 13 How the First 20 Minutes of Your Day Can Set You Up for Success.**
- **Stillman, Jessica, 2016 August 29 The Perfect Wake-Up Playlist, According to Psychology.**
- **Burling, Darryl, 5 reasons your quiet time is best in the morning.**
- **Awaken, 2018 August, How Journaling Can Help you Heal.**
- **The Charlene Show, 6 Morning Habits for Weight Loss with Shawn Stevenson. Episode 306, Itunes. 2018 June 4**

About

Awake My Soul Ministries

CorrieLeeAnn is the daughter of an Evangelist Missionary and Gospel Singing family. After a lifetime of ministry, singing with her family, and her 10 years of work in the field of education, she began to desire ways to combine her love for teaching and sharing God's love through music. In January of 2019, Corrie began the Awake My Soul ministry. This ministry creates faith-based resources designed around the concept of encouraging today's Christian woman toward dependence, wholeness and identity with her Creator. Corrie's debut program is entitled The AWAKE, 5 step morning routine. This is a routine designed to encourage women towards a lifestyle of "centered in Christ" wholeness. Visit our website at www.corrieleeanns.com for more information about products and workshops that Corrie is currently hosting. If you are in need of an event speaker, consider CorrieLeeAnn for your next women's event.